JUNIOR'S

Activity Book

DAVE RAMSEY'S
financial peace
JUNIOR

Published by Lampo Press, The Lampo Group, Inc.
Brentwood, Tennessee 37027

Lesson One:

WORKING

Junior washes dishes every day to help earn his commission money.

LESSON ONE: **WORKING**

Hi, friends! I'm Junior. Welcome to *Financial Peace Junior*! In this activity book, you will learn four important lessons about money: working, giving, saving and spending. Don't worry! I promise that we'll have plenty of fun along the way. In Lesson One, we'll talk about **WORKING** to make money. Are you ready for our first adventure? Let's go!

Do you have chores that you have to do at your house? I do. I help clean up the kitchen after meals. I make my bed every morning. And I do my homework without being asked. These are things I do just because I'm part of a family. I don't get paid for them.

A few years ago, my mom told me that I could start earning commission for extra chores I do around the house, like cleaning my room, helping with the laundry and taking out the trash. She explained that commission is money you make for working and doing chores.

I was so excited. Making my own money sounded like fun! I thought of the things I could buy with the money I earned: movies, video games and cool toys.

My mom and dad sat down with me to explain how it all worked. They gave me a chore chart, which I keep on the refrigerator. Whenever I finish a chore, I mark it off. On Friday—PAYDAY!—my mom and I add up all the chores I do for the week, and she pays me in cash! It is an awesome feeling to know I work hard to earn my commission. And it's so much fun to dream about what I want to buy with the money I earn.

Making money and doing the right things with it takes a lot of discipline and hard work. But I can tell you from experience, it pays off! You will feel so proud knowing that you earned your commission. And you will soon be on your way to becoming a successful money manager. That's right! It doesn't matter if you are eight years old or 80 years old. You can learn how to handle money and make it work for you! Cool, huh?

HOW IT WORKS

Keep track of your chores using your chore chart. Place a check beside each chore as you complete it. You can even write the amount you get paid beside each chore. On payday, it's important to immediately put your commission money in your envelopes.

TRY THIS

On Saturday, Dollar Bill helped his mom **dust** the furniture in the living room and dining room. He made **$1**. He helped his dad **clean** and organize the garage for **$5**. Then, he helped his mom **carry in groceries** and put them away while she cooked dinner. He made **$2**. How much did Dollar Bill earn that day?

Helpful Hint: Use your calculator to add the total of Dollar Bill's commission.

______ + ______ + ______ = $ ______

(Dust) (Clean) (Carry Groceries) Dollar Bill's Commission!

WRAPPING IT UP

Hi, I'm Esther! Did you know that working hard is important in all areas of life? It is! We should always do the best we can in everything that we do.

"In all the work you are doing, work the best you can. Work as if you were doing it for the Lord, not for people."

Colossians 3:23 (NCV)

LESSON ONE: **WORKING**

Help Junior find the way to his commission money by going through the maze of chores.

WORKING

Junior feels proud of himself when he does grown-up chores like vacuuming the carpet.

LESSON ONE: **WORKING**

Junior loves to do **chores** to **earn** his **commission money**. He puts away his **clothes**, helps **sweep** the floor, folds **laundry**, **washes** the **dishes**, and **cleans** his room. Junior gets **paid cash** for his **work** every **week**.

Find the **bold** words from the sentences above in the Word Search below.

I	J	E	N	W	E	C	W	C	E
D	S	K	C	H	A	O	E	P	S
Y	E	E	R	S	Y	O	E	H	N
R	H	R	H	O	E	E	K	C	C
D	T	O	M	S	W	D	N	H	A
N	O	I	S	S	I	M	M	O	C
U	L	N	R	A	E	D	S	R	M
A	C	U	P	W	A	S	H	E	S
L	I	J	C	L	E	A	N	S	A
E	I	S	H	N	H	E	A	O	I

❍ Junior
❍ Chores
❍ Earn
❍ Commission
❍ Money

❍ Clothes
❍ Sweep
❍ Laundry
❍ Washes
❍ Dishes

❍ Cleans
❍ Paid
❍ Cash
❍ Work
❍ Week

WORKING

Junior's hard work pays off every week on PAYDAY!

LESSON ONE: **WORKING**

Write down a list of chores that you can do around the house to earn commission money. Here are some hints to help you think of ideas. Fill in the blank next to each word with as many chores as you can think of.

1. Wash ___________________________
2. Dry ___________________________
3. Clean ___________________________
4. Wipe ___________________________
5. Put away ___________________________
6. Pick up ___________________________
7. Dust ___________________________
8. Mop ___________________________
9. Sweep ___________________________
10. Sort ___________________________

Now, show your list to your parents and decide together what chores you will do. Then, you can write them on your chore chart and begin completing them. You will soon see how fun it is to work hard and earn money for yourself!

Lesson Two:

GIVING

Junior is a cheerful giver with a generous heart.

DAVE RAMSEY'S financial peace JUNIOR

LESSON TWO: **GIVING**

Hi, friends! It's me again—Junior! Great job finishing Lesson One. I hope you are excited about working and earning commission. Now, are you ready to learn about **GIVING**? Okay. Let's jump in to Lesson Two!

A few years ago, one of my friends couldn't afford to go to summer camp. His dad lost his job, and they were having a hard time paying their bills. I didn't want to go to camp without my friend, so I decided that I would give some of my commission each week to help pay his camp fee. I told my parents about it, and they offered to match the money I gave. Then, a few more friends decided to help. We all worked really hard to raise the money. We even had a car wash in our church parking lot.

By the time we left for summer camp, he had all the money he needed to pay for it. We had so much fun together at camp, and it wouldn't have been the same if he hadn't been able to go. That experience taught me to not only think of myself and the things I want to buy with my money, but to also think of others.

Sometimes, giving is hard when we have worked so hard for our money. But if we remember that we are blessed with so much, it is easier to give just a small portion of what we earn to help others. When we do this, a strange thing happens. It feels good! Our hearts become less selfish because we are thinking of others instead of ourselves. And that is always a good thing!

HOW IT WORKS

First, decide where to give and how much. Then, place that money in your GIVE envelope. For example, if your total commission is $5, multiply 5.00 (5 dollars) x .10 (10 percent). Your total giving will be: .50 (50 cents)! Place 50 cents in your GIVE envelope and take it to church or give it to a charity.

TRY THIS

In one week, Dollar Bill made **$12 commission** doing chores and helping with other projects.

Dusting: $1
Putting Away Groceries: $2
Taking Out Trash: $1
Cleaning Garage: $5
Cleaning Bedroom: $2
Washing and Drying Dishes: $1

TOTAL: $12

He is going to **give 10%** to the offering at his church. How much will his total giving be?

Helpful Hint: Use your calculator and multiply Dollar Bill's total **commission** for the week by **10% (.10)** and that's how much Dollar Bill gives.

________________	x	.10	=	$ ________________
(Total Commission)		(10%)		Dollar Bill's Giving!

WRAPPING IT UP

Hi, it's me, Esther again! If you are thankful for everything that you have, it will be easy to give away some of what you earn to help others. Then you can truly be a cheerful giver.

"God loves a cheerful giver."
2 Corinthians 9:7 (NKJV)

LESSON TWO: **GIVING**

There are a lot of kids who don't have everything that they need. Sometimes, they need help from other people for things like food and clothes.

Giving to others makes us less selfish and helps people in need.

What does Junior give to the boy to help him? Circle the things that are different in the second picture.

GIVING

Junior gives by volunteering his time to serve food to others in need.

LESSON TWO: **GIVING**

Junior loves **helping people** in **need** by **giving food**, **clothes** and **toys**. He also puts **money** in his GIVE **envelope** to give to his **church** each week. Junior is a **cheerful giver** with a **generous heart**.

Find the **bold** words from the sentences above in the Word Search below.

O	E	D	I	L	N	T	J	T	N
L	S	G	O	G	O	U	H	R	N
U	N	E	N	Y	N	S	E	A	R
F	P	N	S	I	E	I	H	E	E
R	E	E	O	H	P	N	V	H	V
E	O	R	T	E	R	L	O	I	I
E	P	O	L	E	V	N	E	M	G
H	L	U	C	H	U	R	C	H	J
C	E	S	F	O	O	D	E	E	N
O	T	F	N	C	E	V	S	E	T

- ❍ Junior
- ❍ Helping
- ❍ People
- ❍ Need
- ❍ Giving
- ❍ Food
- ❍ Clothes
- ❍ Toys
- ❍ Money
- ❍ Envelope
- ❍ Church
- ❍ Cheerful
- ❍ Giver
- ❍ Generous
- ❍ Heart

GIVING

Junior knows that it feels better to give than to receive.

LESSON TWO: **GIVING**

Here's a giving challenge for you. Ask your parents to help you go through old clothes and toys that you don't use anymore. Put them in a box and take them to a local charity or orphanage to donate to children in need. Then, in the space below, write about your giving experience.

- What kinds of things did you give?
- Who did you give to?
- How did it make you feel?
- Was it hard letting go of your things?
- Do you think it feels better to give than to receive?

How I GAVE:

____

____

____

____

____

____

Lesson Three:

SAVING

Junior enjoys saving his commission money rather than spending it right away.

DAVE RAMSEY'S financial peace JUNIOR

LESSON THREE: **SAVING**

Hi, friends! It's me—Junior! Have you ever wanted a toy so much that you dreamed about getting it? I have! And guess what? I had to save for it. It seemed like saving took forever, but I did it! And **SAVING** was so worth it! Let me tell you about it.

Last year, I wanted a new bike really bad. I asked my parents for it for my birthday. When my birthday party was over, I was disappointed that I didn't get it. I told my dad that I was sad about not getting the bike, and he explained that it was a little expensive and a lot for our family to spend on a birthday gift. Then he suggested that I save my commission to buy the bike myself.

I really wanted it right then, so I asked my dad if I could borrow the money from him to buy it. Then, each week, I could pay him back. He told me that borrowing money is never a good idea. He even taught me a Bible verse: "The borrower is the slave of the lender" (Proverbs 22:7, NRSV). He explained that we should always HAVE money before we SPEND money, and that borrowing leads to trouble. I agreed to save until I had the money to buy the bike. We figured out how many weeks it would take for me to save enough, and every Friday on payday, I put more money in my SAVE envelope. I could hardly wait for payday the last week. On Saturday morning, my dad took me to the store and I paid for the bike with cash. I had worked so hard and waited a long time, but I finally did it. I rode my bike all weekend, and I was so proud of it. And guess what? I love my bike even more because I saved and bought it myself!

HOW IT WORKS

Once you add up your commission each week and subtract your giving, you can decide how much of your earnings you want to save. For example, if you have $4 left over each week after giving, and you want to buy a $12 toy, how many weeks will you need to save to buy it? Divide 12 (12 dollars) ÷ 4 (4 dollars). You get 3, right? It will take you three weeks to earn enough to buy the toy.

TRY THIS

Dollar Bill is saving for a **$35 toy**—a cool Video Spy Watch! He cut out a picture of the watch from a toy catalog and put it on his chore chart next to his savings goal.

Each week, he makes a **$10 commission** for doing chores and helping around the house. He **gives 10%** of his earnings (**$1**) to the offering at church. Then, he likes to **spend $2** each week on candy or snacks. How much does that leave him for saving each week?

Helpful Hint: Subtract Dollar Bill's giving and spending from his weekly commission.

__________ - __________ - __________ = $ __________

(Commission) (Giving) (Spending) Dollar Bill's Savings!

Finally, if he is saving for a **$35 toy**, how many weeks will he need to save to buy it?

Helpful Hint: Use your calculator and divide **35** by his weekly **savings** (the number you wrote in the blank above). This is how many weeks Dollar Bill will need to save before he can buy the Video Spy Watch.

$35 ÷ __________ = __________

(Spy Watch Cost) (Savings) # of Weeks to Save!

WRAPPING IT UP

Hi, it's me, Esther again! If you can save money, it shows that you are growing up and becoming more mature. Way to go!

> "On the first day of every week, each one of you should put aside money as you have been blessed. Save it up so you will not have to collect money after I come."
>
> 1 Corinthians 16:2 (NCV)

LESSON THREE: **SAVING**

Junior has saved a lot of money, but it's hidden in his room. Circle as many dollars and coins as you can find in the picture. Now count the money.

1. How many dollars does Junior have? ____________

2. How many coins? ____________

3. If each of the bills equals $1.00, how much money in dollars does Junior have? $ _______

4. If each of the coins equals $.25, how much money does he have in coins? $ _________

5. Finally, add the dollar amount plus the coin amount. How much total money does Junior have? $ __________

SAVING

Saving for something special motivates Junior to work hard.

LESSON THREE: **SAVING**

Junior puts money in his SAVE **envelope** every **week** when he is **paid** his **commission** for **chores**. He **works** hard to **save** his money so that he can **buy** things that he **wants**, like new **toys**! Junior has **fun saving** his **money** because then he **always** has some!

Find the **bold** words from the sentences above in the Word Search below.

G	E	C	H	O	R	E	S	M	S
G	P	V	N	W	O	R	K	S	J
N	O	I	S	S	I	M	M	O	C
I	L	B	Y	E	N	O	M	S	I
V	E	W	A	Y	U	B	T	T	E
A	V	S	I	P	J	N	O	N	I
S	N	A	L	W	A	Y	S	N	S
E	E	V	E	W	S	I	U	I	I
V	J	E	G	S	W	F	D	M	A
Y	K	E	A	O	I	I	S	A	S

❍ Junior
❍ Envelope
❍ Week
❍ Paid
❍ Commission

❍ Chores
❍ Works
❍ Save
❍ Buy
❍ Wants

❍ Toys
❍ Fun
❍ Saving
❍ Money
❍ Always

SAVING

Junior loves watching his money grow!

LESSON THREE: **SAVING**

Saving can be fun, especially when you are saving to buy something you really want! Cut out a picture of a toy or game you want to save for and attach it to your chore chart next to your Savings Goal. Then, each week when you are paid commission for your chores, add money to your SAVE envelope. When you save enough money, reward yourself by buying what you want. You can be proud of yourself for working hard and saving to buy things with your own money!

Junior is saving for a super red racer bike!

- What is the very first thing you want to save for? ______________________________
- How much does it **cost**? ______________________________
- How much can you **save each week** from your commission money? ______________
- How many weeks will you need to save to buy it? ______________________________
  *(Hint: Divide the cost of the item by your **weekly savings** to get the number of weeks it will take to buy it.)*
- Is it hard to wait? ______________________________
- How do you think you'll feel when you can go to the store to buy it? ______________

____

Lesson Four:

SPENDING

Junior finally gets to reward himself by spending some of his commission money.

DAVE RAMSEY'S financial peace JUNIOR

LESSON FOUR: **SPENDING**

Hi, friends! It's me—Junior! Now that we've learned about working, giving and saving, it's time for the fun part: **SPENDING**! Spending can be a lot of fun! But did you know that it also takes work? That's right. Responsible spending takes having a plan.

One summer I wanted to go to the carnival with my friends. I asked for permission from my parents, and they agreed. They told me that I needed a plan for spending my commission money when I was there. We decided that I would need money for rides, food and games. I saved my commission for several weeks, and finally it was time for the carnival. I was so excited!

I separated my money into three different envelopes: rides, food and games. When my friends and I got to the carnival, we headed straight to the games. I really wanted to win a prize, so I took a dollar from my games envelope and began playing one of the games. I didn't win the first time, so the carnival worker told me to try again. I knew I could win, so I tried one more time. Then another. And another. I kept losing, but I really wanted that prize! I kept giving my dollars to the carnival workers and, before I knew it, I was out of game money. I didn't think it would be a big deal if I took some money from my rides envelope, so I borrowed a few dollars from there. Then, before I knew it, that envelope was empty. I told myself I'd just take one dollar from my food envelope. But, I didn't win that game either, so I took a few more dollars. I looked down at my envelopes, and all three of them were empty. I couldn't believe it. I didn't have any money left for corn dogs and cotton candy or for any of the rides. I left the carnival bummed that I spent all of my money in one place. I didn't mean to lose track of my money, but I forgot to remind myself of my plan. And it cost me . . . BIG!

HOW IT WORKS

Now that you have some money in your SPEND envelope, you can decide what you want to spend it on! Make a plan for your money. It helps to write it down so that YOU control where it goes. You can even divide up your SPEND money and put it into different paper envelopes like I did for the carnival. Writing down your spending plan helps you stay on track!

TRY THIS

Dollar Bill wants to go to a movie with his friends and decides to make a plan with his money. He's been putting **$5 a week** in his SPEND envelope for **3 weeks**.
How much does Dollar Bill have in his SPEND envelope?
Helpful Hint: Multiply his weekly spending money by the number of weeks he's been saving.

____________ x ________ = $ ____________
($ put in SPEND envelope each week) (# of weeks) **Dollar Bill's SPEND Money!**

In addition to buying his movie ticket, Dollar Bill wants to buy popcorn, a drink and candy. The **movie ticket costs $6**; **popcorn costs $3**; **a drink costs $2**; and **candy costs $2**.
Helpful Hint: Add the cost of all of the items together.

______ + ______ + ______ + ______ = $ ________
(Ticket) (Popcorn) (Drink) (Candy) **Total Cost!**

Does he have enough in his spend envelope for his plan? __________
Helpful Hint: To find out, subtract your Total Cost from his Spend Money.

________ - ________ = $ __________
(Spend Money) (Total Cost) **Extra Spending Money!**

Did you get a positive number? If so, then Dollar Bill has enough money for this spending plan!

WRAPPING IT UP

Hi, it's me, Esther again! We want to be wise with our money and plan ahead, and we don't want money to control us. Spending money is fun, but it doesn't give us true happiness and contentment. The love of money is not good for us. True happiness comes only from being thankful for what we already have.

"Keep your life free from the love of money, and be satisfied with what you have." Hebrews 13:5 (NCV)

LESSON FOUR: **SPENDING**

Here's a practice challenge for you! Pretend you are going to the county fair with your friends. You have saved $20 in your SAVE envelope. From the list below, choose what things you want to do at the fair. Then, place them in three different categories: games, food and rides.

Giant Pretzel $3
Ferris Wheel $2
Drink $2
Spider Ride $1
Hot Dog $2
Roller Coaster $2

Scrambler Ride $1
Balloon and Dart Game $1
Funnel Cake $3
Tilt-A-Whirl Ride $1
Duck Pond Game $1
Snow Cone $1

Bumper Cars $1
French Fries $2
Milk-Can Toss Game $1
Ring Toss Game $1
Dunk Tank Game $1
Pizza $3

How much will you need to place in each envelope? Add up your total cost for each category, as well as your grand total. (Remember, you can't spend over $20.)

TOTAL: ______________

TOTAL: ______________

TOTAL: ______________

GRAND TOTAL: ______________

SPENDING

Junior likes buying things on sale because then he saves money!

LESSON FOUR: **SPENDING**

Junior thinks spending **money** is **fun**, but it's **more** fun when he has a **plan**. Before Junior **buys** anything, he makes sure that he has **enough** money in his SPEND **envelope**. Then he **decides** if he really wants to buy that **item** or if he would rather **keep** the **cash**. He **knows** that having money doesn't mean you have to **spend** it all! **Saving** is fun too!

Find the **bold** words from the sentences above in the Word Search below.

S	E	D	I	C	E	D	G	K
W	I	T	E	M	D	V	R	N
O	E	E	O	F	U	N	O	D
N	G	N	I	V	A	S	I	N
K	E	P	O	L	E	V	N	E
Y	B	R	P	U	C	R	U	P
D	U	N	O	E	G	A	J	S
E	Y	P	O	M	E	H	S	A
E	S	E	E	A	B	K	N	H

- ❍ Junior
- ❍ Money
- ❍ Fun
- ❍ More
- ❍ Plan
- ❍ Buys
- ❍ Enough
- ❍ Envelope
- ❍ Decides
- ❍ Item
- ❍ Keep
- ❍ Cash
- ❍ Knows
- ❍ Spend
- ❍ Saving

SPENDING

Junior likes to spend some of his money, but not all of it.

LESSON FOUR: **SPENDING**

Spending money is fun, but it's easy to lose track of where we spend it if we don't have a plan! Now that you have money in your SPEND envelope, let's practice making a plan.

1. Step 1: **HOW MUCH** money do you have in your SPEND envelope? $__________
   Your plan can't go over this amount.

2. Step 2: **WHERE** do you want to spend your money? The movies? The mall? The toy store? Write **WHERE** you are going to spend your money here: ______________________

3. Step 3: **WHAT** do you want to buy while you are there? If you go to the movies or a toy store, think about the cost of each **ITEM**. Write how much each of them **COSTS** here:

	ITEM	COST
1)	________________________	$__________
2)	________________________	$__________
3)	________________________	$__________

4. Step 4: Add up the **TOTAL** cost of your items using your calculator. **TOTAL**: $________

5. Step 5: **CHECK** your plan. Your answer for #4 must be LESS THAN or EQUAL TO your answer for #1.

___________	-	___________	=	_____________________
(Answer #1)		(Answer #4)		**Extra Spending Money!**

Do you have a positive number? Great job! Your plan is a success!

6. Step 6: Put your plan into **ACTION**! To help you stick to your plan, divide up your cash into categories using paper envelopes. You will need one for each item. Label them by category and put your cash in each one.

7. Finally, take your envelopes with you to the store, mall or movie theater. Remember, don't take money from one envelope and use it for something else like Junior did at the carnival. Stay on track. You can do it!

Junior's Adventure Books make learning about money fun!

Junior takes his Adventure CDs with him everywhere he goes.

Junior loves to watch his money grow in his GIVE - SAVE - SPEND bank.

YOU DID IT!

Great job! You finished all four lessons and are on your way to becoming a successful money manager. Pat yourself on the back. Handling money takes a lot of hard work, but you can do it! Remember to use the tools in this kit to keep track of your working, giving, saving and spending. Don't beat yourself up if you get off track or mess up. Just try again. It will get easier and easier the more you practice. Finally, HAVE FUN!

Your friend,
Junior

CUT HERE

CONGRATULATIONS!
(CHILD'S NAME)
YOU COMPLETED FINANCIAL PEACE JUNIOR!
ALL THAT HARD WORK AND SAVING PAID OFF. YOU ARE NOW AN OFFICIAL JUNIOR MONEY STAR!
CONGRATULATIONS! I AM PROUD OF YOU!
YOUR FRIEND,
Junior
OFFICIAL JUNIOR MONEY STAR!!
$